ONE SUN RISES

ONE SUN RISES

AN AFRICAN WILDLIFE COUNTING BOOK

Wendy Hartmann • *illustrated by* Nicolaas Maritz

DUTTON CHILDREN'S BOOKS   NEW YORK

Library of Congress Cataloging-in-Publication Data

Hartmann, Wendy.
One sun rises: an African wildlife counting book/by Wendy Hartmann;
illustrated by Nicolaas Maritz.—1st ed.
p.   cm.
ISBN 0-525-45225-7
1. Counting—Juvenile literature.   2. Zoology—Africa—Juvenile literature.
[1. Counting.   2. Zoology—Africa.]   I. Maritz, Nicolaas, ill.   II. Title.
QA113.H38   1994   513.2'11—dc20   [E]   93-49735   CIP   AC

Published in the United States 1994 by Dutton Children's Books,
a division of Penguin Books USA Inc.
375 Hudson Street, New York, New York 10014,
by arrangement with The Inkman, Cape Town, South Africa

Designed by Amy Berniker
Printed in Hong Kong
First Edition
1 3 5 7 9 10 8 6 4 2

For
Werner, Dominique, and Kirstin,
who never mind when I follow the sun.
· W H ·

One sun rises over Africa.

Two kestrels hover in the sky.

Three elephants move like shadows.

Four beetles scurry in the dust.

Five suricates worship the sun.

Six impalas graze nervously.

Seven egrets screech a warning.

Eight lions snarl with hunger.

Nine hyenas snap for their share.

Ten vultures wait.

Ten reed frogs praise the moon.

Nine moths flutter in her light.

Eight bats swoop silently.

Seven crickets sing for a mate.

Six owls watch.

Five mice scamper for safety.

Four genets feed before dawn.

Three spiders spin.

Two fish eagles call.

One sun rises over Africa.

NOTES ON THE ANIMALS IN THIS BOOK

KESTREL • The kestrel is a member of the falcon family. Like all birds of prey, it has a sharp, hooked bill that is good for tearing. It hunts other birds, large insects, and small mammals such as mice. As is true of many birds, the male kestrel is more brightly colored than the female. The rock kestrel is usually seen in pairs. They make their nests on cliffs, ledges, or in hollows.

ELEPHANT • Elephants live in large herds that are usually led by an older female. An elephant's tusks, which grow throughout its life, are actually huge front teeth. Its trunk has many uses: it can serve as a nose, a lip, a hand for gathering food, and a hose for drinking and bathing. Though tremendously heavy and ten feet tall at the shoulder, the African elephant moves easily and very quietly. The elephant's greatest enemy is the human; its survival has been threatened by hunters that kill it for its ivory tusks.

BEETLE • There are at least 250,000 species of these insects throughout the world. Two commonly found in Africa are the dung beetle and the rhinoceros beetle. These beetles roll their food into a ball and bury it for themselves and their larvae. The beetle has a set of hard, leathery front wings that are used not to fly but to protect its second pair of wings.

SURICATE • Also called the meerkat, this small, burrowing animal is related to the mongoose. It is fond of company, living in large groups or colonies, and often shares its underground home with other creatures, such as snakes. Suricates like the sun and are particularly active in the early morning and late afternoon, but they must beware of eagles and other predators.

IMPALA • This member of the antelope family is known for its grace and its ability to outjump all other African animals. It can leap over bushes that stand ten feet tall and across streams that are as wide as thirty feet. The impala lives in a large herd that usually can be found near water. The male has long curving horns that serve as weapons.

EGRET • This graceful bird is known for its beautiful feathers, which become even more elaborate during its mating season. The cattle egret is so named because it is found near grazing animals, often on their backs. The cattle egret eats the insects that it finds on the animals—a good arrangement for bird and beast. It also eats spiders, scorpions, frogs, and lizards.

LION • The second-largest cat in the world after the tiger, the lion is now found mainly in Africa. Lions live and hunt in groups called prides. Females do most of the hunting. Only the male has the mane and the powerful roar often associated with lions. Many people understandably fear them, but lions would rather avoid danger than fight. Humans are the biggest threat to this great beast.

HYENA • This doglike animal is a hunter and a scavenger, with excellent senses of sight, smell, and hearing. Its behavior is unpredictable: It may live alone or in packs, and be active during the day or at night. The spotted hyena is also called the laughing hyena because of the noisy whooping, yelling, and giggling sounds it makes.

VULTURE • This large bird may remain in flight for hours at a time, soaring on its long, broad wings. Vultures are found on all continents except Australia and Antarctica. The white-backed vulture is common in southern Africa. In order to find food, it follows other vultures, birds of prey, or predatory animals like lions and hyenas. It then feeds on the body of an animal that these predators have already killed. Vultures rarely kill animals themselves.

FROG • The cold-blooded frog begins life in water as a tadpole but later develops lungs so it can live on land as well. Like other frogs, the reed frog has webbed hind feet and protruding eyes. What makes the reed frog (and its close relation, the tree frog) unusual are the devices on the ends of its fingers and toes, which act as suction cups and enable the frog to hold on to the stems of reeds and other water plants.

MOTH • Unlike their more colorful cousin, the butterfly, moths are nocturnal, flying by night. But like the butterfly, the moth develops in four distinct stages: egg, larva, pupa, and adult. There are as many as 100,000 different species of these scaly-winged flying insects all over the world.

BAT • Though the bat has very poor eyesight, it has no trouble flying at night. Bats use a sonar system to locate solid objects, making high-pitched noises that bounce off the objects in their path. During the day, they hang in trees or attics, or in groups within caves or hollows. Some people are scared by bats, but they serve a very useful purpose: They eat insects, their favorite food.

CRICKET • The characteristic chirp of the cricket is the male insect's way of attracting a female. The male cricket rubs one wing over the other, and the vibration makes this sound. When he feels threatened, the cricket is able to dampen the sound of his chirp so that it is harder for predators to find him. Crickets mostly eat plants and often make permanent burrows for themselves in the ground.

OWL • During the day, owls nest in tree hollows or other dark places. At dusk, they come out to hunt insects, frogs, mice, and small birds. With their keen sense of hearing, owls easily catch their prey in the dark. Soft feathers fringe their wings, so their flight is almost silent. The barn owl, so called because it frequently nests in barns, has light coloring and a white, heart-shaped face. Barn owls can be found on every continent except Antarctica.

MOUSE • Among the smallest of mice are the pygmy mice, which live in grassy or weedy areas. They build round nests, which are located under or on the surface of the ground, from soft grass and other materials. The pygmy mouse eats mostly seeds. Its babies, called pups, are born during the summer months, usually two to five at a time.

GENET • This catlike creature has a pointed face; a long, spotted body; and an equally long striped tail. Genets are good climbers and can often be found in trees, especially when they are hiding from another animal or hunting their prey. Most of their hunting and other activities take place at night, when they prey on small animals and birds. The genet eats insects and wild fruits as well. Though one variety of genet can be found in western Asia and southern Europe, most genets live in Africa.

SPIDER • There are many different kinds of spiders found all over the world. These eight-legged creatures are predators, feeding on the insects they catch in the elaborate webs they spin. The spider produces a special silk for building webs, shelters, and sacs for its eggs. Though some spiders are poisonous, most are harmless.

EAGLE • One of the most striking of these beautiful birds is the African fish eagle. As its name implies, this eagle eats fish, so it is always found near water: rivers, lakes, dams, or the sea. The African fish eagle is also known for its ringing, distinctive cry, which is heard most often at dawn.